Swedish FIKA

Skyhorse Publishing books may be purchased in bulk at special discounts for sales promotion, corporate gifts, fund-raising, or educational purposes. Special editions can also be created to specifications. For details, contact the Special Sales Department, Skyhorse Publishing, 307 West 36th Street, 11th Floor, New York, NY 10018 or info@skyhorsepublishing.com.

Skyhorse® and Skyhorse Publishing® are registered trademarks of Skyhorse Publishing, Inc.®, a Delaware corporation.

Visit our website at www.skyhorsepublishing.com.

10 9 8 7 6 5 4 3 2 1

Library of Congress Cataloging-in-Publication Data is available on file.

Cover design by Daniel Brount
Recipes, text, and styling: Milo Kalén
Photographs and styling: Tine Guth Linse
Graphic design: Edholm & Ullenius
United States unit conversions: Gun Penhoat

Print ISBN: 978-1-5107-6319-7
Ebook ISBN: 978-1-5107-6664-8

Printed in China

Swedish FIKA

CAKES, ROLLS, BREAD, SOUPS, AND MORE

MILO KALÉN

Photographs by Tine Guth Linse

Skyhorse Publishing

tuvwx

56789

EFGH

A dream come true!

I'd just turned fifty-one and felt my time had come. I wanted to realize my dream and open a café where I'd bake just like you do at home—with an open kitchen. I've always loved going into pizzerias where you can see the pizza master at work and can stand and point to the ingredients you want. I wanted that kind of feel!

The three words that guided my search for the perfect premises were warmth, feeling, and experience. Finally, I found it, just a few hundred meters from where we live, a bit hidden and tucked away but still in the center of Limhamn. This was where I was going to open my café! So we got to work. Walls and ceilings were torn down, new tiles and furnishings went up. And I built a kitchen that was fully visible from the café.

My passion for cooking and baking is something I inherited from my mother. She was a pro at making the "seven types of cake and cookies" that are essential for a traditional Swedish fika. And we had lots of fika! Sewing bees, coffee parties, morning coffee, afternoon coffee, evening fika—there was always an occasion to enjoy her fabulous home baking. I didn't do that much baking while I was young and still living at home; it was only after starting my own family that my interest awakened. And you should have seen how much ended up in the trash at first! Everything I made was rock hard and totally inedible! But perseverance paid off, and as my children and their circle of friends grew, so did my fika baking expertise.

In March 2013 it was time to open my very own café! With the sweet smell of buns in the oven and a little help from Facebook and Instagram, the guests started dropping in . . .

When I'm in the kitchen . . .

Flavor comes first,
good ingredients second,
and it has to be fuss-free!

Something I often say when I'm explaining how to make a cake, soup, or bake bread is: "Don't worry about it too much." And you really don't have to—as long as you're enjoying what you're doing. Taste it, feel the consistency, use the ingredients you like, and it'll be great! Be adventurous too. If it fails, well, OK—sometimes you have to throw it away and start again. Then, once you've got the knack, experiment! Knead your dough for a longer or shorter time, make different shapes or add delicious fillings. Try substituting part of the flour with another kind; brush and decorate your pastries with different things. It's about finding your favorites. I love vanilla, which I'm sure you'll notice from the recipes. If it says a teaspoon, I use at least a tablespoon. And rosemary—that must be God's gift to humanity!

I hope this book inspires you to try my favorite recipes and create your own. Play with the recipes—add a pinch of salt or sugar, even if it doesn't say so. Or tip the dough onto an oven tray instead of into a baking pan. Have fun!

Milo

A note from the editor: Both metric and imperial measurements are included in these recipes. In some cases, metric units have been rounded slightly for simplicity.

SHORTCRUST PASTRY

Basic cookie dough

This is a basic dough from which you can make all kinds of different cookies. Here you can see jam thumbprints, currant cookies, Brussels cookies, and Mazarins but you can shape them any way you like and add all sorts of fillings. It's the perfect dough to experiment with!

14 tbsp (200 g) butter left out of the fridge for approx. ½ hour

1²/₃ cups (400 ml) flour
½ cup (125 ml) potato flour
¾ cup (200 ml) sugar
½ tsp baking powder

Put all the ingredients in your Kitchen-Aid bowl or food processor and mix until the dough starts to clump together. You can also mix the dough by hand. Scoop the mixture out onto a pastry board or work surface and knead briskly to form a dough. Leave the dough to rest for about 30 minutes in a cool place (but preferably not in the fridge, which is a little too cold!). Your basic dough is now ready.

Let your imagination run wild!
Once you've made the basic dough, you can roll it however you like and use your favorite flavorings and fillings. Good luck!

Milo fingers

Fork cookies

Jam thumbprints

Brussels cookies

JAM
thumbprints

Makes approx. 50

1 batch shortcrust pastry,
see page 12

½ cup (100 ml) raspberry jam

Set the oven to 350°F (175°C) (convection), or 390°F (200°C) (conventional). Make the shortcrust pastry
according to the recipe on page 12 and
roll the dough into balls, approximately 1¼ inches (3 cm) in diameter.
Put them on an oven tray lined with
parchment paper. Make a well in the
center of each ball with your thumb
but don't press right through the
dough or the jam will run out onto the
oven tray. Spoon raspberry jam into
the wells and bake the cookies in the
center of the oven for approximately
12 minutes.

Two types of
BRUSSELS COOKIE

One with cocoa ... and one without

Makes approx. 50

1 batch shortcrust pastry,
see page 12

approx. 2 tbsp cocoa
¾ cup (200 ml) pearl sugar
a few drops of red food
coloring
1 beaten egg

Make the shortcrust pastry according to the recipe on page 12, adding the cocoa along with the other dry ingredients. Roll the dough into a log, approximately 2 inches (5 cm) in diameter. If you prefer, flatten it a little to make rectangular cookies, like in the picture. Leave the dough to rest in the refrigerator for at least half an hour. Tint the pearl sugar as described below.

Set the oven to 350°F (175°C) (convection), or 390°F (200°C) (conventional). Take the dough log out of the fridge and brush with egg. Pour the colored sugar onto a sheet of parchment paper and roll the log in it. Cut into ⅓ inch (1 cm) thick slices and place on an oven tray lined with parchment paper. Bake the cookies in the center of the oven for approximately 10 minutes.

Makes approx. 50

1 batch shortcrust pastry,
see page 12

¾ cup (200 ml) caster sugar
a few drops of red food
coloring
1 beaten egg

Make the shortcrust pastry according to the recipe on page 12. Roll the dough into a log measuring approximately 2 inches (5 cm) in diameter and store in the refrigerator for at least half an hour. Tint the caster sugar with the food coloring (see below).

Set the oven to 350°F (175°C) (convection), or 390°F (200°C) (conventional). Take the log of dough out of the fridge and brush with the egg. Pour out the colored sugar onto a sheet of parchment paper and roll the log of dough in it. Cut into ⅓ inch (1 cm) thick slices and place on an oven tray lined with parchment paper. Bake at the center of the oven for approximately 10 minutes.

Tinted sugar

Pour a few drops of food coloring onto a dish and add the sugar. Stir it around with your fingers for a while and voilà, pretty tinted sugar!

Fork cookies

Makes approx. 50

1 batch shortcrust pastry,
see page 12
¾ cup (200 ml) raisins

Set the oven to 350°F (175°C) (convection), or 390°F (200°C) (conventional). Chop the raisins and make the shortcrust pastry according to the recipe on page 12 but also mix the raisins into the dough. Roll the dough into balls approximately 1¼ inches (3 cm) in diameter and put them on an oven tray lined with parchment paper. Flatten the balls with a fork, leaving a striped impression, before baking in the center of the oven for approximately 12 minutes.

Milo
FINGERS

This recipe is a simplified version of Milan fingers and a favorite at the café.

Makes approx. 40

1 batch shortcrust pastry, see page 12

1 beaten egg
a few drops of red food coloring
7 oz (approx. 200 g) almond paste
²/₃ cup (approx. 150 ml) pearl sugar
½ cup (100 ml) flaked almonds

Set the oven to 350°F (175°C) (convection), or 390°F (200°C) (conventional). Make the shortcrust pastry according to the recipe on page 12 and roll it out into a rectangle measuring approximately 4-6 inches (10-15 cm) wide and ¼ inch (½ cm) thick. Brush with egg. Knead the food coloring into the almond paste and form a baton as thick as your forefinger and as long as the dough you have rolled out. Place the baton of almond paste along the bottom edge of the dough and roll up lengthwise to encase the almond paste. Press the edges of the dough together and brush with beaten egg. Sprinkle pearl sugar and flaked almonds onto a sheet of parchment paper and roll the dough in the mixture. Cut the dough into pieces about 1½ 2 inches (4-5 cm) long. Place on an oven tray lined with parchment paper and bake in the center of the oven until golden brown (approximately 12 minutes).

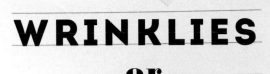

WRINKLIES
or
jitterbugs

In Sweden, these cookies are usually known as jitterbugs but my mum used to call them "wrinklies." The number of times I've heard guests at the café sigh and say, "These are so hard to make!" But they're not. The problem might have something to do with being too careful. The dough is quite messy but no matter how "ugly" the cookies look on the tray, they sort themselves out in the oven and come out all wonderfully wrinkly!

Makes approx. 40

1 batch shortcrust pastry, see page 12

1 egg white
⅜ cup (100 ml) caster sugar

Set the oven to 350°F (175°C) (convection), or 390°F (200°C) (conventional). Make the shortcrust pastry according to the recipe on page 12 and roll it out into a rectangle measuring approximately 8 inches (20 cm) wide and ¼ inch (½ cm) thick. Whisk the egg white until stiff and slowly pour in the sugar while you continue to whisk. Spread the meringue mixture thickly over the entire rectangle of dough. Use a spatula to help you fold in one of the long sides, rolling up the dough like a Swiss roll. Cut the roll into ⅔-1¼ inches (2-3 cm) thick slices and place cut-side up on an oven tray lined with parchment paper. Bake in the center of the oven until golden, for approximately 10 minutes

Have a nice sit down . . .

The oven is yawning with a smile—it's been awake a long
time, checking out the scene:
Kneading and baking to the heat of the oven
and the clang of the kitchen;
To the beat of the sputtering coffee machine.

Soon all the ingredients will have fallen into place,
Waiting to be tasted when the door opens,
When the first footsteps arrive.

They keep coming in; cups and plates descending on
tables, coffee-thirsty folks keep opening the door
And the clock keeps ticking happily:
just a drop more, please!

At noon, lunchtime hunger sets in
Then a potpourri of everything and everyone, sitting,
laughing, and smiling;
An extra bit of cheese with that slice of bread,
A nice cookie taken by the hand
And the piece of pie that speedily needs to occupy a
ravenous thought.

At last, four o'clock and the door shuts goodbye
Only to open tomorrow with freshly baked warmth
And the promise of another delicious day!

Stellan Hökfelt

Mazarin cake

1 batch shortcrust
pastry, see page 12

about ⅜-⅞ cup (100-200 ml)
raspberry jam
4½ oz (125 g) almonds
9 tbsp (125 g) softened
butter
2 eggs

Glaze

1¼-1²/₃ cups (300-400 ml)
confectioners' sugar
a dollop of raspberry jam
a few drops of water

Set the oven to 355°F (180°C) (convection), or 400°F (205°C) (conventional). Stick a sheet of parchment paper to the bottom of a springform pan; you don't need to grease the sides. Press the dough into the pan, allowing it to reach approximately 3 cm up the sides. Spread raspberry jam over the bottom. Grate the almonds in a nut grinder. Mix the butter, grated almonds, and eggs in a mixing bowl and spoon the mixture over the bottom, carefully distributing it over the raspberry jam. Bake in the center of the oven for approximately 30 minutes. Let the cake cool before prising it out of the pan. Pour the confectioners' sugar into a mixing bowl and mix with the raspberry jam to make a pale pink glaze. If it gets too dry, add a few drops of water, but it should be thick when it's ready. Pour the glaze over the cake and spread carefully with a spatula. Serve with a dollop of lightly whipped cream.

Psst!

Look out for a nut grinder the next time you're at a flea market. They are indispensible for cookie baking!

Instead *of*
GINGER SNAPS . . .

**Swedish pepparkakor (ginger snaps) should be super thin, but
I don't really have the patience for that so I usually make these
instead. They're delicious and extremely easy!**

Makes approx. 40

6 tbsp (100 g) softened butter
⅜ cup (100 ml) sugar
¼ cup (50 ml) light syrup*
1 tsp ground cinnamon
1 tsp ground ginger
½ tsp ground cloves
3½ oz (100 g) flaked almonds
1¼ cups (approx. 300 ml) flour
½ tsp baking soda

*You can substitute Lyle's Golden Syrup or molasses.

Put butter, sugar, and syrup in a bowl and use an electric whisk to beat until fluffy. Mix the spices, almonds, flour, and baking soda in another bowl and then stir into the mixture.

Whisk again to form a crumble and then press the dough together with your hands. Tip the dough onto a floured surface and make a roll, approximately 1¼ inch (4 cm) in diameter. Flatten the roll to make it rectangular and wrap in plastic wrap before leaving to chill in the refrigerator for at least 4 hours. Heat the oven to 350°F (175°C) (convection), or 390°F (200°C) (conventional). Take out the dough and cut it into thin slices with a really sharp knife.

Put the slices on an oven tray lined with parchment paper and bake at the center of the oven for 10-12 minutes. Allow the ginger snaps to cool before storing in a jar.

Psst!

The old "coffee cup" measure is roughly ⅔ cup (150 ml).

Grandma's cookies
or Swedish
BISCOTTI

**My grandma used to bake these little rusks, and
then my mother after her. It was also the thing
that got me liking coffee. I would sit on Grandma's
lap and dip the rusk in her coffee . . .
a fond childhood memory.**

Makes approx. 40

10½ tbsp (150 g) softened butter
1 coffee cup (⅔ cup) caster sugar
1 heaped coffee cup (about ⅔-¾ cup) almonds
1 egg
3½ coffee cups (about 2⅓ cups) flour
1 tsp baking powder

Garnish

1 beaten egg
2 tbsp caster sugar
2 tbsp grated almonds

Set the oven to 350°F (175°C) (convection), or 390°F (200°C)
(conventional). Grate the almonds in a nut grinder. Quickly
whisk all the ingredients together in a mixing bowl. Scoop
the dough out onto your work surface and shape into three
long rolls, each measuring approximately 1¼ inch (4 cm) in
diameter. Put the rolls on a cookie sheet lined with parchment paper and flatten them a little. Brush with the beaten
egg before mixing the sugar and grated almonds and sprinkling
over the rolls. Bake in the center of the oven until golden
brown (approximately 15 minutes). Remove the rolls and reduce
the oven temperature to 165°F (75°C) (convection), or 215°F
(100°C) (conventional). Cut the rolls diagonally into pieces
that are approximately ¾ inch (2 cm) wide and arrange on the
oven tray cut-side up, leaving them to dry in the oven for
at least 1 hour. Store the biscotti in an airtight jar. Best
enjoyed dipped in hot black coffee!

Fina's
SYRUP SLICES

I got this recipe from my best friend, Fina. When my kids were small, my own recipe for these cookies just wasn't good enough—it had to be Fina's! The number you make depends on how large you cut them.

Makes approx. 40

14 tbsp (200 g) butter (not straight from the fridge)
¾ cup (175 ml) sugar
1 tbsp pale syrup (or Lyle's golden syrup)
2 tbsp vanilla sugar
2 cups + 3 tbsp (500 ml) flour
2 tsp baking powder

Set the oven to 350°F (175°C) (convection), or 390°F (200°C) (conventional). Cut the butter into small pieces. Mix everything together as much as possible in a bowl before scooping the dough out onto a pastry board or your work surface. Knead it together with your hands. Divide the dough into three pieces and roll them out to fit the length of your baking sheet. Arrange the dough rolls on the sheet (lined with parchment paper) and flatten. Bake at the center of the oven for approximately 15 minutes.

Take out the baking sheet and diagonally cut the cookie lengths while still warm. Allow to cool before removing from the baking sheet.

Oat lace COOKIES

These crispy little, leaf-thin lace cookies are something I often rustle up when I realize I've forgotten to make dessert. Served with vanilla ice cream and warm berry compote, they're a luxurious treat!

Makes approx. 15

5¼ tbsp (75 g) melted butter
⅜ cup (100 ml) sugar
⅜ cup (100 ml) rolled oats
⅜ cup (100 ml) all-purpose flour
¼ tsp baking powder
1½ tbsp (¼ dl) milk
1½ tbsp (¼ dl) light syrup*

*You can substitute Lyle's Golden Syrup or molasses.

Set the oven to 350°F (175°C) (convection), or 390°F (200°C) (conventional). Mix the sugar, rolled oats, all-purpose flour, and baking powder in a mixing bowl. Add the milk, syrup, and the melted butter. Quickly mix together and use a teaspoon to spoon out onto baking sheet lined with parchment paper. Leave some space between each cookie because the mixture will spread out quite a lot. Bake at the center of the oven until golden brown, for about 10-15 minutes. Allow to cool before removing from the baking sheet.

COCONUT TOSCA

**In Sweden, tosca (croquant) is a favorite sweet topping for
cakes and buns. This tray cake is delicious
and easy to make!**

14 tbsp (200 g) butter

4 eggs

2 cups + 3 tbsp (500 ml) sugar

1¼ cups (300 ml) flour

2½ tsp baking powder

⅞ cup (200 ml) cocoa

2 tsp vanilla sugar

pinch of salt

Tosca topping

7 tbsp (100 g) butter

1 cup + 3 tbsp (250 ml) sugar

⅜ cup (100 ml) pale syrup*

²/₃ cup (150 ml) cream

⅞ cup (200 g) shredded coconut

*You can substitute Lyle's Golden Syrup or molasses.

Set the oven to 390°F (200°C) (convection), or 435°F (225°C) (conventional). Melt the butter in a saucepan and whisk the eggs and sugar to make a batter.

Mix the flour, baking powder, cocoa, vanilla sugar, and salt in a bowl. Pour the flour mixture into the batter and stir. Finally, pour in the melted butter and stir until you have mixed everything thoroughly. Pour the mixture into a baking sheet lined with parchment paper and bake at the center of the oven for 10 minutes.

Make the tosca topping while the cake is in the oven. Melt the butter in a saucepan and mix in the sugar, syrup, and cream, letting the mixture simmer for a few minutes. Stir in the coconut and bring to a boil again, stirring all the time.

Remove from the heat. Take the cake out of the oven and carefully pour the tosca over it. Bake for another 10 minutes or so until the tosca is golden.

Allow the cake to cool before cutting into even-sized pieces. Store the cakes in a tub in the refrigerator—they taste best chilled.

MAMA'S
sponge

A classic sponge cake that you can turn into whatever you like! How about pear tosca, or rhubarb or plum cake? I'm sure you can come up with loads of your favorite fruit and berry combos.

2 eggs
1⅓ cups (250 ml) sugar
7 tbsp (100 g) butter
1⅔ cups (400 ml) flour
2 tsp baking powder
⅜ cup (100 ml) water

Set the oven to 350°F (175°C) (convection), or 390°F (200°C) (conventional), and grease and flour a cake pan. Whisk the eggs and sugar until fluffy. Melt the butter in a saucepan. Quickly stir the flour and baking powder into the egg mixture. Pour the water into the melted butter and then stir this into the mixture. Pour the finished cake batter into the pan. Bake the cake in the bottom half of the oven for 30-45 minutes.

Pear TOSCA

1 batch sponge batter, see page 43
3-5 pears

Tosca topping

10½ tbsp (150 g) butter
²/₃ cup (150 ml) sugar
3 tbsp cream
3 tbsp flour
5¼ oz (150 g) almonds, roughly chopped

Set the oven to 350°F (175°C) (convection), or 390°F (200°C) (conventional). Make the mixture according to the recipe on page 43. Line the bottom of a springform pan (approx. 11¾ inches or 30 cm in diameter) with a sheet of parchment paper—you don't need to grease the sides. Pour the mixture into the pan. Cut each pear into roughly 8 wedges (there's no need to peel the pears). Tightly arrange the pear wedges on top of the mixture. Bake the cake in the bottom half of the oven for approximately 30 minutes.

Make the tosca topping while the cake is baking. Melt the butter in a saucepan and mix in the other ingredients. Simmer for 3 minutes, stirring all the time to prevent the mixture from burning at the bottom.

Take the cake out and carefully spread the tosca topping over it. Bake for an additional 10 minutes or so until the tosca is nice and golden. Allow to cool a little before serving.

FRUIT
or
BERRY CAKE

1 batch sponge batter, see page 43

fruit or berries, e.g. rhubarb, raspberries,
apples, or nectarines
2/3 cup (150 ml) crème fraîche
2 tsp vanilla sugar
2 tbsp sugar
juice of half a lemon, if desired

It's difficult to say how much fruit you need—it's a question of preference. I think it's nice to cover the entire cake. If you're using rhubarb, you need to cut it into pieces (around 1/3 inch or 1 cm is good). You can cut apples or nectarines into thin wedges or pieces—it doesn't matter. Experiment!

Set the oven to 350°F (175°C) (convection), or 390°F (200°C) (conventional), and make the mixture according to the recipe on page 43. Line the bottom of a springform pan (approx. 11¾ inches or 30 cm in di-ameter) with a sheet of parchment paper, but you don't need to grease the sides. Pour the mixture into the pan.

Mix your choice of fruit or berries with the crème fraiche, vanilla sugar, and sugar. Spoon this mixture over the cake batter and sprinkle a tiny amount of sugar on top. Sometimes I also squeeze half a lemon over the top.

Bake at the center of the oven for approximately 30-40 minutes. Allow to cool slightly before serving.

Banana cake

**This banana cake is so delicious that even
people who don't like bananas love it!**

3-5 bananas
1 large egg
$^2/_3$ cup (150 ml) milk
⅜ cup (100 ml) crème fraîche
3 tbsp canola oil
1½ cups (350 ml) all-purpose flour
¾ cup (200 ml) sugar
2 tsp baking powder
2 tsp vanilla sugar
pinch of salt
butter, brown sugar, and salt flakes for
the cake pan

Set the oven to 350°F (175°C) (convection), or 390°F (200°C) (conventional). Line the bottom of a springform pan (approximately 9½ inches or 24 cm in diameter) with a sheet of parchment paper and grease it generously with the butter. Dust the pan with brown sugar and a scattering of salt flakes.

Peel the bananas and halve them lengthways. Place them cut-side down into the pan, covering the whole base with bananas.

Mix the egg, milk, crème fraîche, and oil in a mixing bowl and all the dry ingredients in another. Fold the dry ingredients into the egg mixture and stir quickly to make a smooth batter. Pour the mixture over the bananas and bake at the center of the oven for approximately 30-40 minutes. Allow the cake to cool a little before turning it upside down onto a dish—tap the bottom of the pan to loosen the bananas. Leave to cool completely and serve with lightly whipped cream.

Carrot CAKE

Virtually all cafés in Sweden now serve carrot cake—perhaps it's the easiest way of getting our kids to eat root vegetables? I've simplified the recipe to make it easier to memorize.

3 large carrots (approx. ½ lb or 300 g)
3 eggs
1¼ cups (300 ml) sugar
1¼ cups (300 ml) flour
3 tsp baking powder
2¼ tbsp (33 ml) canola oil

Frosting

3½ oz (100 g) cream cheese
4 tbsp (60 g) softened butter
1²⁄₃ cups (400 ml) confectioners' sugar
grated zest of 2 limes

Set the oven to 350°F (175°C) (convection), or 390°F (200°C) (conventional), and line the bottom of a springform pan with a sheet of parchment paper. You don't need to grease the sides.

Peel and grate the carrots. Whisk the egg and sugar until fluffy with an electric whisk. Stir in the flour and baking powder and then the carrots and oil, mixing to a smooth batter. Pour the mixture into the pan and bake in the bottom half of the oven for approximately 30 minutes. Allow the cake to cool before loosening from the pan.

Whisk the ingredients for the frosting with an electric whisk until smooth. Place the cake on a dish and spread the frosting over the cake.

If you prefer, you can make the cake a day in advance and prepare the frosting just before serving.

LEMON
and
LIME PIE

Serve this pie with lightly whipped cream and homemade raspberry jam—yum! Fresh strawberries are great too.

Pie crust

1¼ cups (300 ml) all-purpose flour
1½ tbsp sugar
9 tbsp (125 g) butter
1 egg yolk

Filling

3 eggs
⅞ cup (200 ml) sugar
⅞ cup (200 ml) cream
2 tbsp all-purpose flour
1 tsp vanilla sugar
juice and grated zest of 1 lemon
juice and grated zest of 1 lime

Set the oven to 350°F (175°C) (convection), or 390°F (200°C) (conventional). Line the bottom of a springform pan with a sheet of parchment paper. You don't need to grease the sides.

Put the flour, sugar, and butter on your pastry board and chop it together with a knife—or you can pinch the mixture with your fingers to make a crumbly mass.

Mix the egg yolk in last and knead to form a small dough ball. Press the dough into the pan, pushing it up the sides a little to make a pastry shell. Whisk the eggs, sugar, cream, all-purpose flour, and vanilla sugar in a mixing bowl. Thoroughly wash the lemon and lime and grate the zest. Squeeze the juice from both fruits and add with the zest to the mixture.

Pour the mixture into the pastry shell and cover with a lid or some foil. Bake in the center of the oven for 30 minutes. Remove the lid/foil and leave the pie in the oven for a few more minutes to brown a little. Allow to cool before removing from the pan, and serve with lightly whipped cream and raspberry jam or fresh berries.

FAVORITE
cheesecake

Base

12 digestive biscuits*
5 tbsp (75 g) melted butter
2 tbsp sugar
1 egg

Filling

15¾ oz (450 g) cream cheese
1¹/₅ cups (250 ml) sugar
1 tsp vanilla sugar
3 eggs
grated zest of 1 lemon
2 cups (450 ml) crème fraîche
1¼ cups (200-300 ml) raspberry jam

*You may substitute graham crackers.

Crumble the biscuits—I usually put them in a mixing bowl and crush them with a pestle. You can whiz them in a mixer, if you prefer.

Pour the sugar and melted butter into the biscuit crumbs and stir (continue with the mixer, if using). Mix in the egg.

Line the bottom of a springform pan with a sheet of parchment paper. You don't need to grease the sides. Press the crumb mixture into the pan, pushing it up the sides a little. Refrigerate the crumb mixture while you make the filling. Set the oven to 320°F (160°C) (convection), or 365°F (185°C) (conventional).

Whisk the cream cheese smooth with an electric whisk, pouring in the sugar and vanilla sugar while you do so.

Mix in one egg at a time and continue whisking until everything is well mixed. Add the lemon zest to the mixture, and quickly stir in the crème fraîche. Pour the filling into the pan and bake at the bottom of the oven for 50-60 minutes. The cake should be a bit wobbly when you take it out—it will firm up as it cools.

Once completely cool, spread a nice even layer of raspberry jam over the top.

PRUNE PIE

This pie is very special to me. All my aunties baked it, just like my mum. When I was a child, I liked it best when it came straight out of the freezer. My recipe has lemon in it to add a little acidic contrast to the sweetness.

Filling

9 oz (250 g) prunes
¼-½ cup (50-100 ml) sugar
½ cup (100 ml) water
2 tbsp potato flour, dissolved
in 3 tbsp (50 ml) water

Pastry

2 cups (450 ml) flour
1½ tsp baking powder
½ cup (100 ml) sugar
8½ tbsp (125 g) butter
$^1/_3$ cup (100 ml) milk
1 beaten egg
1 tbsp cream

Boil the prunes, sugar, and water over low heat for approximately 30 minutes. Squeeze in a little lemon and thicken the prune mixture with the potato flour and water to make a really thick cream. Allow to cool.

Set the oven to 390°F (200°C) (convection), or 435°F (225°C) (conventional). Mix the flour, baking powder, and sugar in a mixing bowl. Cut the butter into small pieces. Pinch the butter into the flour mixture and then add the milk. Work to a dough. Scoop it out to knead on the work surface, if necessary.

Divide the dough in two pieces, one slightly larger than the other. Roll them both out and put the larger one in a rectangular oven dish (approx. 11¾ × 9½ inches or 30 × 20 cm) with parchment paper at the bottom. The pastry should cover the whole base of the dish, and can even hang out a little over the sides. Pour the cooled prune cream into the pie shell and cover with the smaller piece of pastry. Fold the overhanging pastry edges on top to "seal" the pie. Prick the pastry lid with a fork. Whisk the egg and cream and brush the pie with the mixture. Bake at the center of the oven for approximately 30 minutes.

Allow the pie to cool before cutting into pieces. Serve with cream or try eating it semi-frozen!

STARTA DAGEN
PÅ
kaka på kaka

♡

Nyhet **GRÖT**

Havregrynsgröt med
spännande tillbehör!
Tex. "Härgjord" sylt torkad
frukt jordnötssmör bär mm......
skapa din egen favorit

KAKAS FRUKOSTPAKET

kaffe
morotsfralla
yoghurt med
härgjord granola

BANANA
cake
WITH PALE
CHOCOLATE FROSTING

I think the frosting on this cake should be really pale, like milk chocolate. If you like it darker, just add more cocoa!

$^2/_3$ cup (150 ml) sugar
3 tbsp softened butter
1½ tbsp canola oil
2 eggs
1$^2/_3$ cups (400 ml) flour
2 tsp baking powder
2 tsp vanilla sugar
pinch of salt
4 bananas
¼ cup (50 ml) milk

Frosting

3½ oz (100 g) cream cheese
4 tbsp (60 g) butter
1$^2/_3$ cups (400 ml) icing sugar
1 tsp cocoa (or according to taste)

blueberries to garnish

Set the oven to 350°F (175°C) (convection), or 390°F (200°C) (conventional). Line the bottom of a springform pan (approximately 9½ inches or 24 cm in diameter) with a sheet of parchment paper.

Mix the sugar, butter, and oil together before stirring in one egg at a time and then mixing in the dry ingredients. Mash the bananas with the milk in a bowl, and add to your mixture. There's no need to stir too much.

Pour the batter into the pan and bake the cake at the center of the oven for approximately 40 minutes. The cake should rise in the middle. Allow to cool in the pan before turning out onto a dish. Mix the ingredients for the frosting with an electric whisk and beat until completely smooth. Spread the frosting over the cake and garnish with blueberries.

ALMOND
cake

This is my daughter Clara's show-stopper—and a given on the menu when she helps out at the café.

5 egg whites
⅞ cup (200 ml) sugar
5¼ oz (150 g) almonds

Buttercream

12¼ tbsp (175 g) softened butter
5 egg yolks
⅔ cup (150 ml) sugar
⅔ cup (150 ml) cream
pinch of salt
1-2 tsp vanilla sugar
⅔ cup (approx. 150 ml) flaked almonds

Set the oven to 340°F (170°C) (convection), or 385°F (195°C) (conventional) Whisk the egg whites until stiff in a clean, dry stainless steel bowl. If you have to make do with a plastic one, give it an extra wipe with a clean, dry tea towel to remove any grease.

Add the sugar a little at a time and whisk until you have a nice, firm meringue batter. Grate the almonds in a nut grinder and fold them into the mixture with a spatula.

Spread the mixture to make two round meringue bases, each measuring approximately 11¾ inches (30 cm) in diameter. Make each one on separate sheets of parchment paper. Bake at the center of the oven for 20 minutes until the bases are a nice color. You can bake both at the same time in a convection oven; otherwise bake each one separately.

Cube the butter and place on a dish. Mix the egg yolks, sugar, and cream in a thick-bottomed saucepan. Put the pan over a medium to high heat and start whisking, continuing until the cream has thickened. Remove the saucepan from the heat and continue to whisk while you add the butter, a little at a time. Whisk until the butter has completely melted. Add salt and vanilla sugar and allow the cream to cool.

Remove the meringue bases from the parchment paper and spread half the buttercream on one. Sandwich together with the other base and spread the remaining cream on top.

Lightly toast the flaked almonds in a dry, nonstick pan. Sprinkle the toasted almonds over the cake and leave in a cool place until it is time to serve. Chilled whipped cream is delicious with this!

French CHOCOLATE CAKE

This delicious chocolate cake is inspired by the one served at the Rosendal café in Stockholm, but we've tweaked the recipe here and there to create our own. It's a rich, wonderfully chocolaty cake, and the use of good quality cocoa is important. Choose your favorite cocoa and adjust the amount to suit you. Wrapped in aluminium foil, this cake will keep fresh for a week.

14 tbsp (200 g) butter
4 eggs
2⅓ cups (550 ml) sugar
4 tsp vanilla sugar
1⅔ cups (400 ml) cocoa
1¼ cups (300 ml) all-purpose flour
pinch of salt flakes

Ganache

3½ oz (100 g) dark chocolate
⅜ cup (100 ml) whipping cream

Set the oven to 350°F (175°C) (convection), or 390°F (200°C) (conventional). Line the bottom of a springform pan with a sheet of parchment paper—you don't need to grease the sides. Melt the butter. Whisk the eggs and sugar in a mixing bowl. Stir in the dry ingredients and finally, the slightly cooled butter.

Spread the mixture over the base of the pan and bake in the center of the oven for approximately 15 minutes. Take out the cake and leave to cool.

Meanwhile, make the ganache. Finely chop the chocolate. Heat the cream in a saucepan, remove the saucepan from the heat, and add the chopped chocolate. Stir until the chocolate has fully melted. Spread the ganache over the cake and leave to set. Serve small slices of the cake with lightly whipped cream, if desired.

Basic
BUN *dough*

You can make lots of delicious things with this basic sweet dough recipe.

Makes 20-25 buns

2 packets (14 g) active dry yeast
12¼ tbsp (175 g) butter
2⅕ cups (500 ml) milk
pinch of salt
⅔ cup (150 ml) sugar
6 cups (approx. 1400 ml) all-purpose flour, divided

Crumble the yeast in the bowl of your mixer, if using. Melt the butter in a saucepan, switch off the heat, and pour in the milk. Check the temperature with a thermometer or do the finger test—the liquid should be max 100°F (37°C). Pour a little of the dough liquid onto the yeast and stir until the yeast has dissolved. Now add the rest of the dough liquid, along with the salt, sugar, and half of the flour.

Work in the rest of the flour, a little at a time, until the dough loosens slightly from the sides of the bowl. I usually work the dough for 5 minutes in the machine, but it will take longer by hand. Dust your fingers with flour and check the consistency of the dough—it shouldn't stick to your finger, but almost.

Detach your bowl, sprinkle the insides with a little flour, and cover with a clean tea towel. Leave to proof for approximately 30 minutes.

Cinnamon BUNS
and more

1 batch of dough according to the
recipe on p. 69

Filling

16½ tbsp (250 g) butter, softened
⅞-1 cup (200-250 ml) caster sugar

vanilla sugar according to taste
cinnamon, freshly ground cardamom,
or raisins

or:
1⅕ cups (250 ml) crème fraîche
2 tbsp vanilla sugar

Brush and garnish with:

1 beaten egg
pearl sugar

Scoop the dough onto a lightly floured surface. Roll the dough with a light hand, gently pressing outwards to form a rectangle. If you don't have much space, split the dough in two and make two batches. Spread on the butter and sprinkle over the sugar.

Now decide how to flavor the buns—I always use vanilla sugar, then sprinkle on cinnamon, freshly ground cardamom, or raisins. Sometimes, I mix crème fraîche with vanilla sugar, spread this thinly over the dough, and sprinkle over raisins—it's really delicious. Try out your own combinations! Roll up the rectangle lengthways to make a long snake, and position it seam-side down. Cut the snake into evenly sized pieces and place cut-side up into bun cases on an oven tray. Leave to proof under a proving cloth for 30 minutes. Set the oven to 390°F (200°C) (convection), or 435°F (225°C) (conventional).

Brush the buns with beaten egg and sprinkle over pearl sugar. Bake in the center of the oven for approximately 10-15 minutes.

Butter cake
or wreath

Make the dough as previously described (p. 69) but instead of putting the buns in cases, place them together in a greased springform pan to make "butter cake". Be careful not to squash them together too much. Leave to proof in the pan under a tea towel for approximately 30 minutes. Set the oven to 350°F (175°C) (convection), or 390°F (200°C) (conventional). Bake in the lower half of the oven for approximately 30 minutes.

Or...

Roll out, fill, and roll up the dough. Place the "snake" on a sheet of parchment paper on an oven tray, joining both ends of the snake to make a wreath. To create the plait effect, use scissors to slash halfway through the dough and fold each cut piece alternately right and left (see picture). Leave to proof on the tray under a tea towel for approximately 30 minutes. Set the oven to 365°F (185°C) (convection), or 410°F (210°C) (conventional), and bake in the bottom half of the oven for approximately 30 minutes.

FOCACCIA

This bread is fabulous with soup or salad. To achieve the chewy consistency of focaccia, the dough has relatively little flour in it and has to be kneaded for quite a while, so use a machine if possible. Experiment with toppings to suit you!

Makes 1 focaccia

1 packet (7 g) active dry yeast
2$^{1}/_{5}$ cups (500 ml) lukewarm water
1 tbsp salt
½ cup (100 ml) sesame seeds
4¼ cups (1 L) durum wheat flour, divided
½ cup (100 ml) olive oil
¼ cup (50 ml) oil
black olives
2 tbsp dried rosemary
salt flakes

Pour or crumble the yeast in a mixing bowl and pour in the water. Mix until the yeast has dissolved. Add the salt and sesame seeds and stir in half of the flour. Add the oil, and then work in the rest of the flour. Work the dough in your machine for around 10 minutes. Leave to proof under a tea towel for about 30 minutes before rolling out.

Oil an oven tray or large oven dish and scoop the dough onto it. Flatten the bread with your hands until it is approximately ⅓ inch (1 cm) thick. Use your fingers to press a few holes into the dough and leave to proof under a clean tea towel for approximately 30 minutes. Set the oven to 390°F (200°C) (convection), or 435°F (225°C) (conventional).

Drizzle a little oil over the bread and sprinkle on olives, rosemary, and salt flakes. Bake in the bottom half of the oven for approximately 30 minutes.

Tip!

Experiment with diffe-
rent toppings for the
focaccia. For example,
sliced red onion or
sun-dried tomatoes
are delicious!

CARROT
bread rolls

These soft moist rolls have become a classic at our café, Kaka på Kaka. Fill them with cheese, ham, Dijon mustard, lettuce, and tomatoes for a deliciously filling lunch sandwich!

Makes approx. 16 rolls

3¼ tbsp (50 g) butter
2$\frac{1}{5}$ cups (500 ml) milk
1 packet (7 g) active dry yeast
3 tbsp dark syrup (or treacle/light molasses)
1 tbsp salt
3 cups (700 ml) sifted rye flour
1 lb 1 oz (500 g) grated carrots
3 cups (700 ml) all-purpose flour
beaten egg
pumpkin seeds

Melt the butter in a saucepan and pour in the milk. Heat to 100°F (37°C)—you can use a thermometer or test with your finger. Pour or crumble the yeast into the bowl of your mixer and pour on the liquid, stirring until the yeast has dissolved. Pour in the syrup (molasses) and salt and mix in the rye flour. Leave the machine to work the dough for a while. Grate the carrots and mix them into the dough. Add almost all the flour, a little at a time, and continue working the dough in the mixer for approximately 5-10 minutes. If the dough feels too sticky, you can add a little more flour but it mustn't get dry.

Powder a little flour around the dough and leave to proof under a tea towel for 30-40 minutes. Set the oven to 390°F (200°C) (convection), or 435°F (225°C) (conventional).

Tip the dough onto a floured surface and divide into two lengths with a spatula. Divide each length into 7-8 pieces and put the pieces cut-side up on an oven tray lined with parchment paper. Leave to proof for a further 30 minutes under a tea towel.

Brush with beaten egg and sprinkle over the pumpkin seeds. Bake at the center of the oven for approximately 15 minutes. Allow to cool on a rack, under a tea towel.

Bread
in a jar!
Mix all the dry ingredi-
ents in a jar and write
a note with things that
need to be added.
Makes a lovely
present!

KAKA PÅ KAKA'S
rustic loaf

This bread contains quite a lot of different ingredients, so while I'm making it, I prepare several batches of the dry ingredients and put them in plastic bags. When I get round to baking again, all I need to do is add the sour milk and carrots.

2 loaves

$2^1/_5$ cups (500 ml) all-purpose flour
$1^2/_3$ cups (400 ml) rolled oats
$1^1/_5$ cups (250 ml) sifted rye flour
$1^1/_5$ cups (250 ml) whole wheat flour
½ cup (100 ml) whole or crushed flaxseeds
½ cup (100 ml) sesame seeds
½ cup (100 ml) pumpkin seeds
½ cup (100 ml) sunflower seeds
1 tbsp salt
4 tsp baking soda
4¼ cups (1 L) Swedish filmjölk or buttermilk
2 large grated carrots
butter and rolled oats for the bread pans

Set the oven to 375°F (190°C) (convection), or 420°F (215°C) (conventional). Grease two bread pans and dust with rolled oats.

Thoroughly mix the dry ingredients in a mixing bowl (or bags or jars if you're preparing a bread mix to save for later). Next, stir the buttermilk and carrots into the bowl and pour the batter into the pans. Sprinkle on your choice of seeds and bake at the center of the oven for approximately 90 minutes.

Tip the bread straight out onto a rack and allow to cool without covering. Store the loaves covered with a tea towel, and once you've started cutting one, keep it cut-side down on a plate (not in a plastic bag) to preserve the delicious crust. The bread will keep fresh for several days.

RYE RINGS

These wonderfully chewy bread rings are perfect filled with smoked salmon, cream cheese, and lettuce—a bit like bagels! Alternatively, try spreading on mayo, lettuce, a fried egg, and tomato, or toast the bread and top with cheese and marmalade.

Makes 12-16

1 packet (7 g) active dry yeast
2½ cups (600 ml) warm water, about 100°F (37°C)
2 tbsp dark syrup (or treacle/light molasses)
1 tbsp salt
3 cups (700 ml) sifted rye flour
1⅕ cups (250 ml) rolled oats
1 egg
2⅕ cups (500 ml) all-purpose flour

Crumble or pour the yeast into the bowl of your mixer. Pour the water over the yeast and stir until the yeast has dissolved. Add the syrup and salt and mix in the sifted rye flour, rolled oats, and egg. Finally, work in the flour a little at a time. Work the dough in the machine for approximately 5 minutes. Since the dough is quite sticky and difficult to combine, a dough hook is really handy here. Sprinkle some flour around the dough and leave to proof for 30 minutes.

Set the oven to 365°F (185°C) (convection), or 410°F (210°C) (conventional). Tip the dough out onto a floured surface. Divide into 12-16 pieces and shape each one in your hands to make a flat bun measuring approximately 4 inches (10 cm) in diameter. Pinch a hole in the middle of each bun with your thumb and forefinger and arrange them side by side on an baking sheet lined with parchment paper. Leave to prove under a tea towel for 30 minutes. Bake at the center of the oven for approximately 10-15 minutes until lightly golden.

JAM

This is embarrassingly easy! I always make fairly small batches of jam so that I can use less sugar (most jams need a lot of sugar to preserve them for longer). The result is a much tastier jam and I use it all up before it has a chance to go moldy. I love making nectarine marmalade, but you can concoct your own favorites!

1 lb 2 oz (500 g) fruit or berries,
fresh or frozen (defrosted)
⅞ cup (approx. 200 ml) jam sugar, more if the
berries/fruit are acidic

optional: boil with a vanilla bean
or cinnamon stick

Rinse the fruit or berries. Peel and core the fruit and cut into pieces. I often don't bother with peeling if the fruit is organic and skins are in good condition. Put the berries or fruit in a thick-bottomed saucepan and mix in the jam sugar. Stir over low heat to dissolve the sugar, and allow to boil for at least 5 minutes or until the fruit/berries are reasonably soft. Keep stirring as you do this.

Pour the jam into clean jars and store in the refrigerator. The jam will keep for about a month—just check its appearance, taste, and smell to make sure it hasn't gone bad!

Tip!

Add a few drops of
lemon to the warm jam
for more acidity.

PICKLED
red onion and fennel

A tasty accompaniment for hamburgers, pulled pork, or salads. The recipe uses "1-2-3" proportions for the pickling liquid, and you can put whatever you like in it—experiment!

½ cup (100 ml) distilled
white vinegar (12%)
⅞ cup (200 ml) sugar
1¼ cups (300 ml) water

To pickle: 2-3 red onions
or 1 large fennel bulb

Mix the vinegar, sugar, and water in a saucepan and bring to a boil. Remove from the heat and stir until the sugar has melted.

Thinly slice the red onion or fennel. Place in a jar and pour on the slightly cooled pickling liquid. Screw on the lid and leave to cool completely before storing in the refrigerator. The pickle will keep for at least a week.

PESTO

1¾ oz (50 g) fresh basil
1 clove of garlic
pinch of salt
½ cup (100 ml) pine nuts
1¹/₅ cups (approx. 250 ml) grated Parmesan
⅞ cup (200 ml) olive oil

Whiz the basil, garlic, salt, and pine nuts
in a mixer to make a smooth paste. Add the
grated Parmesan and drizzle in the oil, a
little at a time, mixing everything thoroughly. Store in a sealed jar in the refrigerator. Pouring a little extra oil on top
of the pesto in the jar helps it keep fresh
for longer.

Use the pesto...

with freshly made pasta, soups, as a salad dressing or on toasted sandwiches with tomato and mozzarella.

havregryn solrosfrö sesam
linfrö pumpafrö russin
aprikos Granola rapsolja
tranbär cocosflingor
ingefära appeljuice honung
kanel kärlek. V

GRANOLA

Granola is great to make at home because you can add all your favorite ingredients. Here's my version.

4¼ cups (1 L) rolled oats

½ cup (100 ml) each of:
flaxseeds
sesame seeds
pumpkin seeds
sunflower seeds
1 tbsp cinnamon or crushed
cardamom
½ cup (100 ml) canola oil
¼ cup (50 ml) honey
½ cup (100 ml) concentrated apple
juice
⅞ cup (200 ml) coconut flakes

Additionally, a handful of:
raisins
dried cranberries
dried ginger
dried figs
dried apricots

Set the oven to 390°F (200°C) (convection), or 435°F (225°C) (conventional). Pour the rolled oats, flaxseeds, sesame seeds, pumpkin seeds, and sunflower seeds onto a baking sheet lined with parchment paper. Sprinkle with cinnamon or cardamom, drizzle over the oil and honey, and pour on the concentrated apple juice. Mix everything together and roast at the center of the oven until golden (approximately 15-20 minutes). Monitor this carefully and stir the mixture occasionally so that the granola browns evenly and does not burn. Remove the tray from the oven and allow to cool.

Lightly toast the coconut flakes in a dry pan. Chop the dried fruit and berries and add them with the coconut flakes to the granola once completely cool. Store in a sealed jar. This is a really luxurious topping for your breakfast yogurt or oatmeal!

PIMP
your porridge!

Oatmeal porridge—a simple and delicious Swedish classic. Use your favorite brand of oats, and why not add a pat of butter occasionally for a real treat? Go wild with the toppings, of course!

You might like to try these toppings:
jam
peanut butter
honey
cinnamon
dried or fresh fruit
fresh berries

Mix ½ cup (100 ml) rolled oats and ⅞ cup (200 ml) water in a saucepan. Add salt and allow to boil for a few minutes until the porridge is nice and thick, stirring occasionally. Plate up the porridge and pimp with your favorite toppings!

TOMATO SAUCE

You can vary and add to this tomato sauce as much as you like. Have it with pasta or as a BBQ accompaniment, or blend and dilute to make a soup, as on page 102. Use fresh or canned tomatoes, but if you're using fresh ones, roast them in the oven first for the best flavor. And the better the tomatoes, the better the finished result!

Serves 4

2 (14-oz) cans of tomatoes (preferably organic plum tomatoes)
or 2¼ lb (1 kg) fresh tomatoes
1 onion
1 clove of garlic
4 tbsp good olive oil
⅞ cup (200 ml) water
1 vegetable stock cube
salt flakes and pepper
optional pinch of sugar
1 pot of fresh basil

If using fresh tomatoes, you also need:
¼ cup (50 ml) olive oil
salt flakes
dried rosemary
2-3 cloves of garlic

Preparing fresh tomatoes:

Set the oven to 435°F (225°C) (convection), or 480°F (250°C) (conventional). Cut the tomatoes into pieces and arrange on an oven tray lined with parchment paper. Drizzle over ¼ cup (50 ml) olive oil and mix with salt flakes, rosemary, and 2-3 cloves of garlic. Roast at the center of the oven for approximately 30 minutes until the tomatoes have browned a little.

Peel and chop the onion and garlic. Sauté them in the oil in a pan, being careful not to burn the garlic and make it bitter. Pour on the tomatoes—if using canned ones, crush them a little with a fork or cut with scissors. Add the water and crumble in the stock cube. Add salt and pepper and simmer on a low heat for as long as you have time. You can remove the pan from the heat after 15 minutes, but the longer you leave it, the better. I often let mine simmer for hours.

Taste and adjust with a pinch of sugar, stock, or salt, if necessary. Finally, cut the basil and serve with the sauce, grated parmesan, and your favorite pasta, or make the soup on page 102.

Vary your tomato sauce!

Cut mozzarella into small pieces and mix with the pasta and tomato sauce. Serve immediately.

Add olives and chilies for a little more zing.

Add wine instead of water.

Fry some bacon or pieces of chicken and mix into the sauce.

Fry ground beef and add to the sauce to make Bolognese.

Use the tomato sauce on pizza.

The sauce is ideal for freezing—handy when you need to get dinner ready in a hurry!

TOMATO SOUP
with dumplings
AND BASIL OIL

A versatile soup you can get creative with.

Serves 4

1 recipe tomato sauce, see page 97

pinch of chili flakes
½ cup (100 ml) whipping cream

Dumplings

⅞ cup (200 g) flour
3 egg yolks
8 oz (225 g) cream cheese or ricotta
1⅕ oz (30 g) grated Parmesan
salt
a drizzle of oil

Soup

Make the tomato sauce according to the basic recipe on page 97. Add a pinch of chili flakes to lend some comforting heat to the soup. Blend directly in the pot with a hand mixer and pour in the cream. Mix a little more, and then it's ready!

Dumplings

Mix the ingredients together to make a slightly sticky dough. Roll out a finger-thick snake onto a floured surface and cut in pieces approximately 1½ inch (4 cm) wide. Press each one down a little with a fork, if you like. Bring water to a boil in a saucepan—it's good to have one that contains at least 8½ cups (2 L). Add salt. Drop the dumplings into the boiling water. You may have to make two batches, depending on the size of your pan. Boil the dumplings until they float up and remove them with a slotted spoon. Put them in a bowl and drizzle over a little oil to prevent them from sticking together.

Basil oil
Blend ½ cup (100 ml) oil, ½ a pot of fresh basil, and a pinch of salt. Serve the piping-hot soup with the dumplings and drizzle with the basil oil.

CAULIFLOWER
soup
with a STING

**This soup is smooth and creamy but full of character
from the lemon and chili.**

Serves 4

1 large head of cauliflower
2-3 shallots
1 generous tbsp butter
2$\frac{1}{5}$-2½ cups (500-600 ml) water
½ tsp chili flakes
1-2 vegetable stock cubes
1¼ cups (300 ml) crème fraîche
⅞ cup (200 ml) milk
juice of 1 lime or lemon
salt
freshly ground black pepper

Garnish

a few cauliflower florets
2 tbsp canola oil
sesame seeds
chili flakes to taste

Set the oven to 435°F (225°C) (convection), or 480°F (250°C) (conventional). Arrange the cauliflower florets you have saved on a baking tray.

Drizzle over the canola oil and sprinkle on some sesame seeds, along with some chili flakes, if desired. Roast in the center of the oven until the cauliflower is slightly golden. Serve the soup garnished with the roasted cauliflower.

Separate the head of cauliflower into small florets. Peel the shallots and cut into small pieces. Sauté in the butter in a large saucepan. Add almost all of the cauliflower, saving a few florets for garnish.

Pour in the water, add the chili flakes, and crumble in a stock cube. Allow to simmer until the cauliflower is soft, for approximately 15 minutes. Blend the soup and add the crème fraîche and milk. Squeeze in the lemon or lime juice and season with salt, pepper, and more stock, if desired.

Tip!

You can also use sausage or crispy bacon as a topping for the soup.

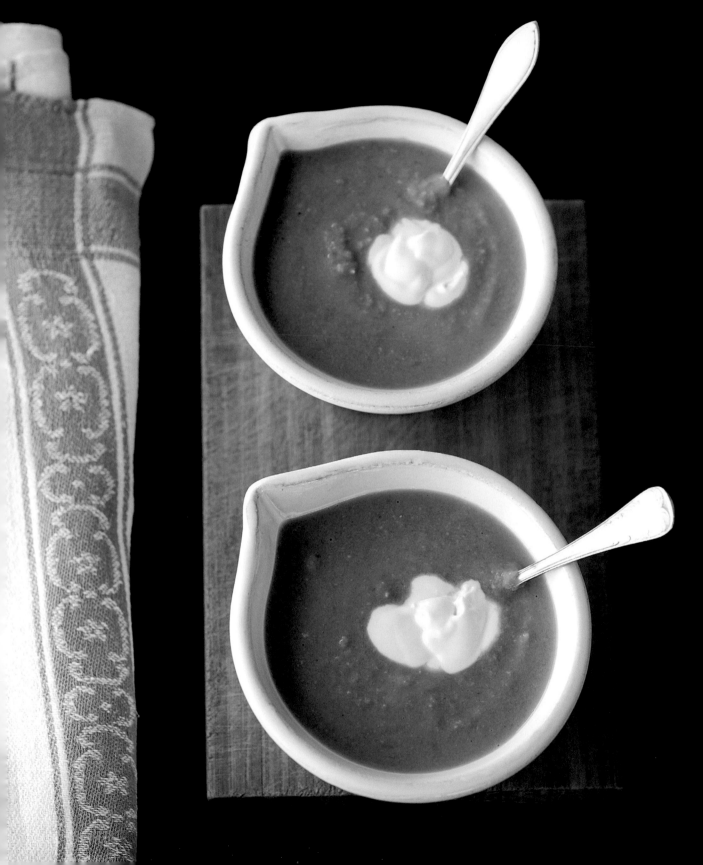

GREEN
pea soup
or CRÈME NINON

A super quick and easy lunch, appetizer, or supper!

Serves 4

2¼ lb (1 kg) frozen green peas
3 cups (700 ml) water
1 tbsp or 1 cube of good vegetable stock
½-⅞ cup (100-200 ml) crème fraîche or cream
salt and freshly ground black pepper

Bring the peas, water, and stock to a boil in a saucepan.
Blend thoroughly, add crème fraîche or cream, and blend a
little more. Season with salt and pepper and serve with a
dollop of crème fraîche. You can top the soup with oven-
roasted air-dried ham for an extra special twist.

Tip!

Mix crumbled goat
cheese with a little
Greek yogurt and spread
on a piece of toast.
Delicious with the
soup!

CARROT SOUP

Serves 4

2¼ lb (just over 1 kg) carrots
4¼ cups (approx. 1 L) water
1 vegetable stock cube
pinch of chili powder
1¹/₅ cups (250 ml) crème fraîche
a few drops of lemon to taste
salt and pepper

Topping

1 carrot
1 parsnip
2 tbsp oil
salt
crème fraîche

Start with the topping. Set the oven to 435°F (225°C) (convection), or 480°F (250°C) (conventional). Peel the carrot and parsnip and thinly shred. Spread the vegetable shreds over an oven tray lined with parchment paper. Drizzle over the oil and add salt. Roast in the oven for a few minutes until nice and golden.

Peel the carrots for the soup and cut into pieces. Place them in a pot and pour on the water to scarcely cover the carrots. Add the stock cube and chili powder, bring to a boil, and simmer until the carrots are soft. Blend the soup smooth, spoon in the crème fraîche, and blend a little more. Season with a few drops of lemon and salt and pepper.

Top the soup with a dollop of crème fraîche and the roasted root vegetable shreds.

TUSCAN
bean soup

Serves 4-6

3 carrots

2 onions

1 small leek

3 sticks of celery

1 small red chili

½ head Savoy cabbage

¼ cup (50 ml) olive oil

½ tsp rosemary

½ tsp thyme

5½-6⅓ cups (1⅓-1½ L) water

2 vegetable stock cubes

1 (14-oz) can white beans

1 (14-oz) can kidney beans

2 fresh tomatoes

or 10 cherry tomatoes

3½ oz (approx. 100 g)

fresh baby spinach

Garnish: Parmesan and fresh thyme

Peel the carrots and onions, and cut into fairly small pieces. Cut the leek lengthways and rinse thoroughly. Chop the leek, celery, and chili into small pieces. Shred the Savoy cabbage. Sauté everything in the oil in a large pot with the herbs. Pour on the water and crumble in the stock cubes. Simmer on a medium heat for approximately 10 minutes.

Drain and rinse the beans in a colander. Add the beans to the soup and simmer for an additional 5 minutes. Cut the tomatoes into medium-sized pieces and add them last, with the spinach. Stir and serve with Parmesan shavings and fresh thyme.

Serve with focaccia!

Focaccia garnished with red onion, rosemary, and salt flakes is delicious with this soup (see page 76 for recipe).

VEGETABLE
gratin
... **HEAVENLY** *and moreish*

I always roast the vegetables in the oven for a while before putting them in the oven dish. It gives them a tender, sweeter flavor.

Serves 4

4 potatoes
½ eggplant
20 button mushrooms
3 carrots
2 parsnips
2 red bell peppers
1 leek
olive oil
salt
2¼-oz (65 g) fresh leaf spinach
1⅕ cups (250 ml) crème fraîche
⅞ cup (200 ml) cream
1⅔ cups (400 ml) grated cheese
(cheddar and mozzarella are tasty)

Set the oven to 390°F (200°C) (convection), or 435°F (225°C) (conventional). Slice all the vegetables but reserve the spinach and put the sliced potatoes to one side. Arrange the other vegetables on oven trays lined with parchment paper. I usually separate each type of vegetable so that if one is ready before the other I can simply take it out and let the rest continue cooking. Drizzle over olive oil and add salt. Roast the vegetables in the middle of the oven until nicely colored, for around 10-20 minutes.

Boil the sliced potatoes in salted water for approximately 5 minutes. Pour off the water and leave the potatoes to steam off a little. Grease a gratin dish and arrange the potato slices at the bottom. Add half of the cheese and then half the spinach. Continue layering with the roasted vegetables, then the rest of the spinach, and finally a layer of potato and the remaining cheese. Whisk the crème fraîche and cream and pour over the gratin. Bake in the bottom half of the oven for approximately 30 minutes, sprinkling on a little extra cheese in the last 10 minutes, if you wish.

Serve the vegetable gratin with a green salad, French dressing, and toasted seeds, or as a meat accompaniment.

STUFFED
tomatoes

If you have any cooked rice left over, this is the perfect way to use it. Otherwise, boil fresh rice and cool before mixing with the filling. I like jasmine rice but short grain works well too. Eggplant, zucchini, mushrooms, leeks, or bell peppers are delicious choices for the filling. Serve with a nice salad or as a meat accompaniment.

For each portion

2 tomatoes
4 button mushrooms and/or your preferred vegetables
oil for frying
2 tbsp grated cheese, e.g. cheddar
⅞ cup (approx. 200 ml) cold boiled rice
1 tbsp pesto
2 slices mozzarella
salt and pepper

Set the oven to 435°F (225°C) (convection), or 480°F (250°C) (conventional). Cut out "lids" from the tomatoes and carefully scoop out the tomato flesh with a spoon. Fry the mushrooms in a little oil and grate the cheese. Mix the mushrooms, cheese, rice, and pesto and season with salt and pepper. Stuff the tomatoes with the mixture and put a slice of mozzarella on each tomato before topping with the "lid." Arrange the tomatoes on baking sheet lined with parchment paper, packing them tightly so that they support each other. Bake at the center of the oven for approximately 30 minutes.

Halloumi BURGERS

You can serve these burgers with mashed potato, potato wedges, rice, or salad, or why not have them as a snack?

Serves 4

4 carrots
2 parsnips
1 eggplant
1 large leek
7 oz (200 g) mushrooms
5¼ oz (150 g) halloumi
1 egg
2 tbsp flour
salt and pepper

Set the oven to 435°F (225°C) (convection), or 480°F (250°C) (conventional). Roughly grate the carrots, parsnips, and eggplant. Cut the leek lengthways and rinse thoroughly. Chop the mushrooms and leek and pile onto a baking sheet. Drizzle with olive oil and roast in the oven for approximately 15 minutes. Remove and allow to cool. Transfer the roasted vegetables to a mixing bowl.

Grate the halloumi and mix it in with the egg. Sprinkle with flour, add salt and pepper, and mix together.

Heat a frying pan with a little oil. Shape the mixture into round burgers—you can flatten them with a spatula in the pan. Fry the burgers on a medium high heat. Try not to turn them too soon—it's easier to prevent them from falling apart once the egg has coagulated and the cheese has melted a little. Three to four minutes on each side usually does the trick.

PRAWN SALAD
Swedish style

A delicious, refreshing, satisfying salad—best made with fresh prawns that you peel at home.

For each portion

⅔ cup (approx. 150 ml) cooked whole grains, e.g. bulgur, pearl barley, kamut
3½ oz (approx. 100 g) cooked prawns
piece of cucumber
½ avocado
1 tomato or a few small ones in different colors
2 cauliflower florets
handful of mixed lettuce

Dressing (per portion)

1-2 tbsp mayonnaise
1 tsp horseradish
1-2 tsp water

Boil the grains according to the instructions and leave to cool. Peel the prawns. Peel and core the cucumber and cut into half-moons. Cut the avocado and tomatoes into wedges and divide the cauliflower into small florets. Put the lettuce on plates and arrange the grains and vegetables on top. Add the prawns. Mix the dressing and drizzle over the salad. Serve with a lemon wedge, sprig of dill, and some good bread.

... and
ASIAN STYLE

For each portion

²/₃ cup (150 ml) cooked pearl couscous
¼ cup (50 ml) frozen edamame
3½ oz (100 g) cooked prawns
piece of cucumber
1 bulb fennel
a small piece of black radish
handful of mixed lettuce
¼ zucchini

Dressing (per portion)

1½ tbsp (25 ml) lime juice
½ tbsp runny honey
½ tsp sesame oil
¼ finely chopped red chili
approx. 1 tsp sesame seeds, black
and white if possible
salt

Boil the couscous and leave to cool. Defrost the edamame—just rinse them in lukewarm water. Peel the prawns. Peel and core the cucumber and cut into half-moons. Thinly slice the fennel and cut the radish into thin batons. Make shavings of the zucchini. Put the lettuce on plates and arrange the couscous and vegetables on top. Whisk the dressing together and mix a little of it with the prawns. Put the prawns on the salad and sprinkle on some extra sesame seeds. Serve with a wedge of lime, the rest of the dressing, and some nice bread.

SALAD
with chèvre
and pan-fried
plums

**I usually assemble this salad straight onto the plate.
I haven't given exact amounts—you can adjust them to
suit you. Serve as a starter or main course.**

For each portion

½ cup (100 ml) cooked pearl couscous
generous handful of mixed lettuce
piece of zucchini
piece of cucumber
1 slice of chèvre
2-3 plums (or 1 nectarine)
1 tbsp butter
2 tsp honey
2 tsp balsamic glaze (reduced balsamic vinegar)
a little water
toasted sunflower and pumpkin seeds
salt and pepper

Boil the couscous and leave to cool. Mix the different salad leaves in a large bowl. I usually have iceberg or romaine lettuce as a base and mix in a few different kinds of smaller leaves. Put the salad on plates and sprinkle over the pearl couscous. Shave the zucchini thinly. Cut the cucumber lengthways, core, and cut into half-moons. Distribute the zucchini and cucumber over the couscous and add a slice of chèvre to each plate.

Halve the plums or nectarine and remove the stones. Fry the fruit halves in a little butter in a frying pan and drizzle over a few drops of honey. The fruit is done once it has browned a little. Add salt and pepper. Arrange the fried plums on top of the chèvre, drizzle over reduced balsamic vinegar (dilute with a little water, if you like), and sprinkle on some toasted sunflower and pumpkin seeds.

Tip!

Nectarines or peaches
make good substitutes
for plums, if you
can't get them.

Cauliflower
salad

**Serve this salad as an accompaniment to meat or fish
or with a tomato and leaf salad. You can prepare
the cauliflower salad in advance.**

Serves 4-6

1 head of cauliflower
2 large bunches of dill
3½ tbsp (50 ml) capers
salt and pepper
sunflower seeds to taste

Dressing

3 tbsp Skåne mustard or other coarse-grained mustard
2 tbsp Dijon mustard
3 tbsp honey
3 tbsp white wine vinegar
3 tbsp olive oil

Whisk together the ingredients for the dressing. Separate the cauliflower into small florets and mix with the dressing. Leave to absorb for at least 30 minutes. Pluck off the dill fronds and roughly chop. Mix the dill and capers with the cauliflower and season with salt and pepper. Sprinkle over some sunflower seeds, if desired.

Index

Bread & buns

Basic bun dough.................69
Butter cake....................72
Carrot bread rolls.............78
Cinnamon buns..................70
Focaccia.......................76
Kaka på Kaka's rustic loaf.....81
Rye rings......................83
Sweet dough wreath.............72
Vanilla and raisin buns........70

Cookies

Biscotti, Swedish
  (Grandma's cookies)..........33
Brussels cookies with cocoa....19
Brussels cookies...............19
Fina's syrup slices............34
Fork cookies...................21
Ginger snaps, instead of.......31
Grandma's cookies
  (or Swedish biscotti)........33
Jam thumbprints................16
Jitterbugs (wrinklies).........25
Milo fingers...................23
Oat lace cookies...............36
Shortcrust pastry,
  basic cookie dough...........12
Syrup slices, Fina's...........34
Wrinklies (Jitterbugs).........25

Pies and cakes

Almond cake....................65
Banana cake with pale
  chocolate frosting...........63
Banana cake....................49
Carrot cake....................50
Cheesecake.....................54
Chocolate cake, French.........67
Coconut Tosca..................41
Favorite cheesecake............54
French chocolate cake..........67
Fruit or berry cake............47
Lemon and lime pie.............52
Mama's sponge..................43
Mazarin cake...................28
Pear Tosca.....................44
Prune pie......................58
Sponge, Mama's.................43

Miscellaneous

Granola........................93
Jam............................86
Pesto..........................90
Pickled red onion and fennel...88
Porridge.......................94

Satisfying meals

Halloumi burgers..............116
Stuffed tomatoes..............115
Tomato sauce, variations......100
Tomato sauce...................97
Tomatoes, stuffed.............115
Vegetable gratin..............113

Soups

Bean soup, Tuscan.............110
Carrot soup...................109
Cauliflower soup..............105
Crème Ninon...................107
Green pea soup................107
Tomato soup with dumplings
  and basil oil...............102
Tuscan bean soup..............110

Salads

Cauliflower salad.............123
Prawn salad Asian style.......119
Prawn salad Swedish style.....118
Salad with chèvre
  and pan-fried plums.........120

Conversion Charts

Metric and Imperial Conversions
(These conversions are rounded for convenience)

Ingredient	Cups/Tablespoons/ Teaspoons	Ounces	Grams/Milliliters
Butter	1 cup/ 16 tablespoons/ 2 sticks	8 ounces	230 grams
Cheese, shredded	1 cup	4 ounces	110 grams
Cornstarch	1 tablespoon	0.3 ounce	8 grams
Cream cheese	1 tablespoon	0.5 ounce	14.5 grams
Flour, all-purpose	1 cup/1 tablespoon	4.5 ounces/0.3 ounce	125 grams/8 grams
Flour, whole wheat	1 cup	4 ounces	120 grams
Fruit, dried	1 cup	4 ounces	120 grams
Fruits or veggies, chopped	1 cup	5 to 7 ounces	145 to 200 grams
Fruits or veggies, pureed	1 cup	8.5 ounces	245 grams
Honey, maple syrup, or corn syrup	1 tablespoon	0.75 ounce	20 grams
Liquids: cream, milk, water, or juice	1 cup	8 fluid ounces	240 milliliters
Oats	1 cup	5.5 ounces	150 grams
Salt	1 teaspoon	0.2 ounce	6 grams
Spices: cinnamon, cloves, ginger, or nutmeg (ground)	1 teaspoon	0.2 ounce	5 milliliters
Sugar, brown, firmly packed	1 cup	7 ounces	200 grams
Sugar, white	1 cup/1 tablespoon	7 ounces/0.5 ounce	200 grams/12.5 grams
Vanilla extract	1 teaspoon	0.2 ounce	4 grams

Oven Temperatures

Fahrenheit	Celsius	Gas Mark
225°	110°	¼
250°	120°	½
275°	140°	1
300°	150°	2
325°	160°	3
350°	180°	4
375°	190°	5
400°	200°	6
425°	220°	7
450°	230°	8